Chiaroscuro

Chiaroscuro

KIMBERLY BECK

RESOURCE *Publications* · Eugene, Oregon

CHIAROSCURO

Resource Publications
An Imprint of Wipf and Stock Publishers
199 W. 8th Ave., Suite 3
Eugene, OR 97401

www.wipfandstock.com

PAPERBACK ISBN: 979-8-3852-1127-2
HARDCOVER ISBN: 979-8-3852-1128-9
EBOOK ISBN: 979-8-3852-1129-6

VERSION NUMBER 111025

For Becky and Nancy,
who heard the song of my poetry before it came to be.

Contents

Acknowledgments

I WOULD LIKE TO thank the editors of the following publications, where several of the poems in this book first appeared. I am also deeply grateful to Bruce Gore for his time, insightful wisdom, and thoughtful review of the first draft of the manuscript.

Solid Food Press: "A Doe Passes," "Myrrh and Aloes," and "Desert Eyes"

Ekstasis: "*La Vie En*"

Clayjar Review: "Robes"

Amethyst Review: "Yesterday's Making," "Mourning Dove," and "*Tektōn*"

The Penwood Review: "Paper Lantern" and "Cherry Blossoms"

The Windhover: "The Eagle"

The Rabbit Room: "Tender Feet"

Summer

MOURNING DOVE

Somehow, your song
is softer, even
than the taciturn shade of your feathers
as they return to your sides, on folded wings.

And somehow, your eyes
are the eyes of a sage, warm
and watered, and closed
above the ink-dark band of your clerical collar.

You are bowed above me, on the branch of a tree
that was not supposed to live.
Its tender arms
are steeples in the dawn-light, and you
are a prayer.

A DOE PASSES

She is
a willow tree at dawn
on the far side of a sheltered clearing,
a collage of cautious lines, sun-flecked,
her summer pelt a forest floor
of dappled light and leaves.

She is
in front of me now,
for a moment, or rather
    less than a moment,
just watercolor eyes
and swaying amber sails, her ears
turning to listen.

Then she is gone, with the leaves.

I wonder if her silence
is the sound of His love.

THE EAGLE

At every angle, his face is hidden from me.
He is perched on the smallest branch
of the largest tree, a poplar so old
that it has surely borne countless names
and countless lives.
His gnarled talons cling
to the frame of its outstretched finger;
in the river below, a refraction
of God's hand, and Adam's.

I crane my neck to seek him—
his shoulders in shadow, sloped beneath
the wild dark of his feathered cloak.
The brume of his tail, an alluvial fan
of cloud-white against the sky, and the leaves.

I trundle around the base of the great tree.
I search for his eyes, but
he is so very far above me, gazing out
at something—
the silver trout beneath the river's surface?
The rustling oaks on the far shore?
His song-shadow, the one so far away,
the one
he shares this home with?

A breeze stirs. The pure, unfettered light
of his feathered crown lifts, suddenly tender,
suddenly wise.
From the forest floor, my neck still craned,
I close my eyes,
I see him.

X

On the sunny slope, it sways, the very last
of its kind.
Its gray bark is cool to the touch, a refrain
beneath the spray-can paint
of a sterile, gown-white *X*.
And scrawled across its neck—
  for good measure—
someone has written,
  Leave.

Somewhere down the trail,
young, timid saplings have been planted.
Their beds are pillowed soil, rich
earth and birdsong, and the care
of many bare hands,
tucking them into the damp, autumn grass.

But this one.
This one, aged tree, perhaps just old enough
perhaps just wise enough
perhaps enough stories, enough scars,
watches from the side, from the bank
of a quiet river.
  Leave.

Alone
and not alone,
it has been left to live.

LOW TIDE

I hear the low tide when he paints.
The bowing of the beach grass, tempest blades
brushing, faces downcast
above the cradled sand.
It is the sound of the sea
in midwinter;
the sound of the river
before dawn, before
the meadowlark sings.

I sit in his studio, the salt-gray of my eyes
ebbing with the stillness, and the breeze.
I hear the low tide when he paints.

SOMEWHERE, SIXTEEN

Somewhere, sixteen
trails in Cascade places
left by rifts and rain, and ashen feet.
They must be quick, must be clever,
  must be afraid
of snapping steel, the silver vines,
the jaws of Thrill.

Somewhere, just an estimate
of sixteen embers, fanned into the mountain air
as twirling cinders, released upon a Breath
  and hushed by dawn, into their dens, their last
    sixteen
      safe places.

POTTERY WHEEL

Sometimes, He is slow
in His making.
There is no sudden speech, no
        "Let there Be"; only
a wheel of wood, and stone, and
terra-cotta, holding its breath
as the clay turns, and tumbles.

But His hands are slow,
like the sea;
slow, as they brush the shore
of the broken vessel, shaping
and reshaping
and letting lie fallow again.

He is slow
in His making of a delicate thing,
meant to be filled,
meant to be emptied,
meant to be held.

FOURTH OF JULY

It is a furrowed, patchwork wound
on the back of a golden ridge, raw
and bare, and ungrafted
as it rasps a cinder-charred sigh
into the downcast wind.

Up there, beneath the fractured arms
of a scorched, skeletal tree,
is an empty burrow
and a gust of scattered tracks, and something
somebody buried.

No homes were lost, only
the homes of so many.

SUNDAYS

On Sundays, the air
purrs in its sleep.
It nestles in the barn aisle
in a basket of hay, where a pool of sunlight
    spills
        from an unfolded window.

SLUMBER-SONG

It is the moment after their running—
    a reprise, following the chorus
of so many mountain hooves
over road, and packed earth, and grass.

It is the pause—
the exhale, the head inclined,
that I step into
and out, across the sand, where they wait.

Then, clasps
and buckles
and weathered straps, my arms
lifting gingerly over their ears
as their honey-warmed eyes begin to close
beneath the sun.

To me, the silence sings
    their slumber-song,
and I listen as I tuck them in.

YESTERDAY'S MAKING

At times, the colors
are slow to wake. He turns them over,
finds their edges with a brush, with a stone
and with the sun, prepares a space.
He lifts a canvas and beneath a window
the threads of yesterday's Making
are feathers in the dawn-light, minerals, and prayer, and dust
rising gold.
He listens to their memory.
He sings them back to the Maker, and waits.

FJORDS, AT 2 P.M.

The wind sighs, and they are
     time,
         slowed,
the wide, sandy strokes
of a sea-grass brush.

Autumn

A GIFT OF LEAVES

They fall.
From the cupped hands of the
maple, they spill, just one
or two at a time, little red sails catching,
and turning, in a laconic pantomime.

Along the winding path, they curl
and fold
and flatten, a hearth-glow of paper cranes
and origami foxes, their tapping
a chorus of heartbeats, and wind.

They are the cold day's
cinnamon spices. They are the autumn-thin
ceramics, the earth-made mugs,
filled, and foamed, and pressed
into our trembling hands.

Today, I cannot bring myself
to step on them.

LA VIE EN

We sit in a bakery, a Maker's space.
It is the color of winter's dawn
when at last, the sun,
humble and having no wick,
breathes upon the snow.

Petals of light descend, drifting
above an Ebenezer of roses
above the lines of our listening hands
above a pâtissier's shoulders; her secret:
    an abundance of butter.

Here, and higher than here,
we are received
even as we learn to receive.

BRIDGE

It is bent over the river.
I see it, trembling
above the unsettled ribbon
of the sky's mirror, which is, today,
without color.

It is a web of cold angles, welded
into the trussed shape of a
straining back, as it braces, its
legs planted deep into a bed
littered with locks, and coins, and
other tossed things.
It is made of steel. Cold, and painted
black.

Beyond it, a cloister of broad-shouldered hills
lies solemn, and sleeping. The mountains
curl themselves around us,
the tails of their valleys dusted
with the winter coat of an early, first snow.
They turn in their sleep
and the sun is a canticle somewhere
above them, gently humming
out of sight.

BLIND IN BETHSAIDA

Around him, the crowd
presses. It is a cacophony of crows,
a tangle of clacking talons
and hissing robes. The dust splits
with the shrieks of empty coffers, as coins
are dropped from sharpened beaks
for bets, and unmet needs.

Then, softly, a hand
in his, the feathers
of a Dove.
A sliver of something warm, something like
the recitations of the leaves, the ones
he has not heard
since he was a boy.

And he is hushed away
from the village, from the noise.
The Dove nestles beside him,
and waits; wings
sifting rain, from sound.

In this unhurried space, there is no
brash breaking, no shards of
pottery
shredding the drawn curtains
of his deep-dark.
There is only the stillness,
and the rain.

It is only here that he can answer the question,
for the first time,
"Can you see?"

MAPLE LEAVES

It is noon, and the air's breath is held
in that crisp stillness, the space between
the long-hand ticking, before
the Great Cold.

Maple trees are steepled along the shore.
They lean in
to offer their season's prayers, one at a time,
leaving wrinkles in the river-blue;
before long, crow's feet crease the edges
of the sky's long reflection.

In the stillness, the trees sigh. Their leaves
        like us
are red in their last, long deaths.
And their prayers
        like ours
are carried by the aged lines
of the listening River.

THE BACK FORTY

Trees, remember
all of those mornings, when you
met me on the trail, before dawn.
Remember the grass, cushioned
in swan feathers of frost;
remember the earth, the cadence of
its breath so slow, in slumber. Remember
the dust, packed with pine needles, and roots,
and rocks.

Trees, remember
that one day, that one
sunrise, the way it
splashed across the sky's canvas in slow motion,
a wakening of watercolor pastels, rising
to bid the night farewell.

Remember
the buck that morning,
the way he burst like a comet
from your hands, just beside me, just
within arm's reach.
He stopped at the crest of the hill,
his visage star-bright, and
looked down at me, as I looked
up at him, and we were still.
And we were still.

Trees, teach me
to remember.

INK

Today, let me listen
as the rain does. Let me lie in the furrows
of the fields, let me hear
the sun-stained pages of the earth
beneath my ear.
They turn with the silt and the willow,
rich ink rising forth, little blots and weeping
where their fingers mirror mine.
Let me listen,
as the rain does.

GRAIN

It spills with the clatter of rain
on a cedar roof,
down into a pan of glacier blue.
I turn it over in my hands, once, twice,
letting the mixture fall, and fill the barn
with the incense of earth, and dust, and tilled crops.

She waits so patiently—
just a flicker of wing-tipped ears
and the drawn sigh of her hooves over the floor
passing, and pausing
in the way of water, and salt, and sand.

I place the grain before her,
settle with my back against the sun-warmed stall.
As her breath shimmers above the pan,
I listen to the sigh of her waves
upon the shore.

RIVER CHOIR

Today, the river
is a fireside ribbon,
fluttering, ever softly, as it folds
below the bridge.
And the maples bend, their shoulders
stooped and sloping, languid arms
made pillows
upon a sandy, shoreline desk.
They are a choir
of inclined heads, silent today,
and sleeping.

GREAT BLUE HERON

I wonder if he does not feel Great today,
    only Blue.

He is the rain yet to fall
from an altostratus cloud,
the long, unbent lines of his legs
drifting below his silhouette like
rivulets on rocks, and windowpanes.

He is that stillness before
the soft patter, before
the song of braille on fallen leaves,
and his face
is tucked away. There, where he waits,
with his regal neck so carefully folded, I
can hear the whispered press
of a child's hand on crinkled paper,
the hope carried in the making
of an origami bird.

Though he does not move, I can see
the sky-shadow of his wings
as he lifts into the sky.
He is still Great
to me.

WELL-MADE (KINTSUGI)

Let your hands listen.
It breaks,
and the breaking is more posture
than sound.

Suddenly, softly sundered,
let it sing against your palm
let it speak,
and remember.

GRANDFATHER AT A DRINKING FOUNTAIN

It is an image smaller
than a thimble:
her hair is a tumble of woodland waves,
a playful cascade in a curtain
tied back as she drinks, and he
is an oak tree above her—shade,
and wide leaves, and roots
holding the world in place—
     a cup of cold water
from a stream.

Then she lifts away, and his branches sway
with a smile.
I am left to wonder
at the tapestry of leaves in their wake.

TEKTŌN

The air turns in a wheel of dust and gold
as it falls through an open window.
His hands leave furrows in the dirt, and
as water forms the clay,
remnants spin around Him, a lingering shimmer
of pensive pirouettes.

The chipped bark of His skin
is scraped, and rugged, and steady
as He moves from shaped earth
to felled tree.
A tangle of driftwood hums
its psalm of war-washed splinters,
of rivers running deep, and desperately
dark.

He listens
with the very tips of His weathered fingers,
        listens
with the dust and the dawn-sun, which
still falls, still spins
from the golden pool of His open window.

He listens, and
His listening Makes.

Winter

POCKET ROCK

Like many of us, she carries
something.
It sits in the pocket of fur
beneath her webbed arms, in that spot
just below her heartbeat:
a smooth, water-dark stone,
its edges softened by years
and years of rushing sand. Today, its shape
is an echo of the graceful silhouette
of a sailboat.

She has carried this little
pocket rock
for ten years. It is a tool,
it is a toy,
and it is a memory, a piece
of the sea she was born in, before
she had to be rescued from her home,
from waters too warm.

We watch from behind the glass
as she floats merrily, in that joyful way that
only otters have—
sometimes spinning, sometimes
still—
but always she carries something,
just below her heart.

ADVENT

It often happens this way:
it snows, and my eyes
are clouds
retreating over the backs
of hibernal peaks,
steep pine-wood slopes, and the rattling sigh
of shale, damp eyelids
deftly closed.

In my blindness, I
wonder
at the Light of the World.

Tell me what a star sounds like
that I may follow, too.

MANGER

Maybe
a lamb in a palm of dust
and piled straw.

Maybe
eyes just old enough to see,
softly closed.

Maybe
velvet ears and valley wool
in letter folds.

Maybe
a stillness, tucked away
beneath a loud-bright Star.

Maybe
this is the way
to listen.

FOXES, AS TOLD BY A WILDLIFE CAMERA

In the fall, she returns
as an unfinished portrait.
Half of her face is ravaged red
and fuchsia, little spots and flecks
of crusted blood, and raw
brow. It is as though
her Painter halted, mid-stroke,
as though the canvas was smeared on one side
by an errant elbow, across and through a pool
of crushed minerals, and ink.

She returns to her den
with only half of her ember-bright fur,
only one soft, amber eye,
only the bell-chime cinders that remain
of her sight.

She sleeps. And wakes. And sleeps.
Sometimes she is alone, but more often now,
her mate is there.
She receives the traces of his
shared light:
soft kisses to her wounds; first bites of prey;
the rise and fall of his sides, poppy-glow and warm,
as he wraps his hope around her.

Outside, the snow
is a quilt.
It is drawn around the shoulders
of their hiding place, a cushion
between their wild home
and a tame, red-stained road.

PAPER LANTERN

When the snow falls,
I cannot see.
There is only the stillness
of an onyx curtain, only the space
between the slumbering ground,
and the exiled stars.

The snow falls, and
I am blind.

But maybe
this is the Light of the World:
a paper lantern, a silent, soft thing;
trembling hands fumbling
over a face of pressed pulp, and
cedar, and string.
I cannot see, cannot feel
the candle within, but somehow, I know
it still glows.

MEMORY (ONE FOR BLAKKEN)

Back then, even the sun
  was still. The very last, velvety
tips of its wings, feathered down from your
withers, down to the dust, down
to the listening earth.

I didn't need to see,
to see it. Instead I closed my snow-eyes, to
  hear the light,
and draped my arms across the ringing slopes
of your wide, mountain-steady back, as
  you slept.

You are still the sun's song, and mine.

LOSING LAZARUS

She falls.
Her robes are sheets of water
in a plume of tattered white, an arrangement
of snowy feathers, fanned about her knees
like the trampled petals of the lily.

She touches the ground
that swallowed her brother, and says,
"Lord, if you had been here . . ."

And she doesn't know it, but
He was.

COLOR

Sometimes, the color of a wound
is gray.
No iris-petal bruise,
no ravine of folded rose,
no shorn meadow, no
poppies in the shade.

Sometimes it's just gray,
and black,
and white,
a fracture of colorless lines,
a painting muted, yet somehow
sharper than light, somehow
the sundering of a desert stone
as we pray for water.

ROBES

His robes were supposed to be white.
They were the lilies, they were
    the sun, the way it breathes
through morning rain
just barely, brightly, near.

But sometimes, His robes are the sand.
They are the grit of the floor
under cracking knees, they are
    the paths we softly sweep,
shallow channels in the desert, alluvial fans
of prayer, and pebbles,
    His parched palms
beneath our splayed hands.

SIMEON

For him, it could have been a Night
just like this one.
The bowed back of the sky,
heavy in slumber, curling away from the
absence of stars, the vacancy
of light.

The pale, hand-hewn stones, scuffed
beneath his shuffling feet, his
fraying robes;
and more, rising solemnly around him, reaching
high, into the shadows, high
above his covered head.

It could have been a Night
just like this one, just like
any of the long-darks
of his many, Deep Winters.

So when the Child was placed,
at last,
in the crook of his bent arms,
perhaps it was not his eyes, but his hands
that allowed him to see in the Dark.

PEN AND INK

When I look up, he is
a drawing on lamplit canvas, the curved lines
from a pen, with oil-based ink.
Dust particles dance
in a pool of conical glow, where the lamplight
spills, and shimmers
in a golden eddy, turning
the wide pages of a watercolor book.
I cannot see his face from here, only
the cross-hatch of his shoulders,
those lines, where they rise above the page,
lifting, and falling, as he reads to us
a children's story.

I wonder if this is the kind of thing
He might have drawn back then, in the sand.

HERON, WHEN IT RAINS

He stands in the river
when it rains.
He is so close, and so
far,
the stilts of his legs propping him up
atop the submerged stones, as though
he walks on water.
The shore is far behind him, and
the sheltering arms of the oaks
fall short, their winter-barren branches
outstretched, patiently waiting
for his return.

Slowly, he lifts his great head, and
the only colors in the world
are those pastel lines of
his silhouette—gray, and blue
and gray again.

The rain falls. I watch him, watching
the river's braille. And the sky
is a bedsheet draped over the backs
of cedar chairs, thin fabric
held down by books, and boxes.

We are in a space known only to us,
and Him.

SLOW

He is not like the other birds.
He does not flick through the trees,
does not spin, does not dive, does not
dance
with the shifting patterns of the sun
and the leaves.

And when the early dawn wakes
over the backs of the snow-bright hills
and the river,
he does not sing.

He is not like the other birds.
He is slow.
Slow, in the way he unfolds
from his customary posture—
that of a letter, unstamped, unsent.
Slow, as he stretches
one leg, then the other,
his neck and torso rocking back
and forward again, in the sunset-creak
of an old wooden chair, an old
cedar porch.

A CANDLE CALLED DESPAIR

The arms of a pine tree bend,
harp-like and soft,
as the flame wavers above an
unlit candle, third
from the left.

With the tree
and the cross
and the stilled voice of
the piano, we
hold our breath.

Three times, the lighter clicks.

A droplet of sunlight falls—
so like rain, somehow,
in the way it unfurls just one
delicate finger,
in the way it makes space
in the silence,
as though it knows its touch
might crush the bruised wick.

We hold our breath; the pine tree looms,
its back against the night,
hoping, perhaps,
to shroud us from the wind.

AFTER

After,
the wine. It pours, tumbling over the cliff
of a clay pitcher, rushing down
and down, until it fills the empty spaces
with another shade of red.

After,
the oil. It is a softer landing, a searching gleam
of pillowed dew drops, gathered
and guided
above the deep-canyon floors.

After,
the honey. It does not pour. It does not search.
It rests, the color of the sun's deep sigh
at dusk, when it is not so bright
and not so loud.

And after all of this, at last,
the linen. It curls, and
the sky's eyes close, and
it is a lamb,
nestled in its sleep.

TENDER FEET

Teach me to walk
with tender feet,
as the wild ones do.

Let me be the cinder-glow
of the fox in her burrow, wreathed
around the honey-spark fur
of her sleeping kits.

Let me be the shaded pools
of the doe's eyes
in winter, when the snow falls,
when the stars lean down to listen,
when the world is darker
and softer
than rain.

Let me be the swallow
after flight, when she is
perched upon the branch
where the petals of the lilacs used to be,
and she is just still, and quiet,
her downy head inclined, as though
she is praying
for their return.

CANVAS

On canvas, the colors turn.
They are the rainwater, they are
the pebbled riverbed.
They are what is left of the corkscrew willow,
the gnarled fingers of its outstretched hands.
They strain to brush the surface, as if to say,
"If I could only
            touch the hem."

Spring

FIRST LESSONS

And now, here you are.
You sit in the saddle
above us, straight-backed
and strong, your red shoes the roots
of your poplar silhouette.
The wind calls, and you spread
your branches, your hands
held aloft to the coming clouds,
and the moment's sun.
The leaves of your fingers
wrap tightly over the reins, a braided tether
of sky, and sea,
and the day is dappled
on your navy sweater. You look up, and smile.
Here you are, teaching us
how to Be.

THE MALLARDS

Beneath a filigree of clouds,
the river falls
from their glistening backs.
They are a choreography
of sand, and rain, and dew,
a dance of pairs and couplets, spinning
below the surface, and rising once again
in a series of gracious, happy bows.

Long after the sun goes down, a part of me
is still on the shoreline,
watching them sway.

THE RESURRECTION (WOUNDS)

He sees them every day.
They are the forked branches of
a lightning storm, a knotted
cartography of red rivers,
a continent
drawn across His back.
They are the canyons
in His wrists, ravines drilled
between cliffs of radius
and ulna, for a river
to flow.
They are the punctured lung,
the open side,
the torn scalp.

Somehow, His wounds
are a part of the Resurrection.
He sees them every day.

DESERT EYES

The sand is the sun's ocean floor,
parting, sides lifted by a sky-tide
to receive Him as He kneels.

Grains stir, honey-coral in a wave
drawn by the branch-light of His fingers
and painted, a salve for the desert eyes
of an outcast.

Scales fall. The sand sweeps,
and listens.
They are out
(outside)
of Time.

CHERRY BLOSSOMS

Her boots are cherry blossoms, tapping
as they fall upon the leaves, as they
carry her across
the wet black of the snowmelt,
the gentle turns in the asphalt path.

She is no taller than a sapling's stem,
but somehow, brighter;
somehow, the glow that dances
above a tiny, braided wick—even
in her burnt-marshmallow puffer coat,
and her woolly leggings,
and her knitted trapper hat.

She trundles along beside her father, mittens
cupped around his two fingers.
The river sings to her, and she points, and
she smiles.

The sun has come out today, for her,
after yesterday's storm.

BASIN

This time, the water
is an early spring rain. It falls
in feathered streams, so slowly
that it is more like dust,
more like leaves,
more like February snow.
It collects in the open, candlelit
palms of a clay basin. The first
droplets reach across the parched surface
in rivulets, so many tender rivers branching,
a pattern reminiscent
of a network of scars.

MYRRH AND ALOES

This is their vesper:
they wrap what is left behind,
what is still, what is empty,
what is true—
and not True.

It is a slow thing, a liturgy:
the turning of linen,
the whispering hum
of hand-spun cloth
as layer
by layer, they cradle Him
in crushed eaglewood
and myrrh
and memory.

Everything they cannot say
is said now, as they bury Him
and the garden-backs bow with them
in prayer.

BREAD

It is a mystery to me.
The sun has yet to wake, and
The worn, time-weathered planks
of the cypress table
come together in the spotted dark, a
Jackson Pollock
of flour, and salt, and seed.

His sleeves are rolled back
in pleated wrinkles, pale wisps of cloud
above the dirt and dark of His
sunburned, artisan hands.
And His palms are sailboats, rocking
back and forth
as He kneads the dough.
It is quiet, patient work. It is
an impression of waves,
a silhouette of sea foam,
a memory of water, lapping
against a listening shore.

THE WELL, AT NOON

Tell me about these stones.
Tell me about the ones
with the chiseled lines,
with the sand-worn fractures,
with the crescents left by many buckets,
and many hands,
and many ropes.

Tell me about this water.
Tell me about the reflection
in the deep-dark, the way it
blinks up at you, here, at noon
as though it is a little sad,
as though it is the only person in town
who sees your eyes.

Tell me about this Man,
the One who is tired,
the One who is thirsty,
who knows everything
about everybody, who knows
all you have ever done,
        ever done,
                ever done.

Tell me about Him.
Tell me about the One who
looks at you
as though He is a little sad, as though
He is the only Person in the world
who sees your eyes.

THE ACCIDENT

How can I measure
the weight of your life?

Metal bends
in canyon-river blue,
cracked, and caked
with mud.
And the light is distorted,
dimming
in the twisted face of a broken door.
How much force does a life carry behind it?

A man straddles the dust
and sage, his shoulders
midnight under the sun, arms
straight, and sure.
I cover my ears, but
the velocity of lead
and copper splits in an echo
that shatters my bones,
with yours.
What song of stream
and meadow
welcomed your birth?
And what of your fawns—
the ones you carried, or
never had the chance to?

You have no grave, so
I will bury you here,
inside of me,

in a quiet place with
lilacs, and daisies.
Forgive me.
I cannot measure your life, but
I can cherish it.

TICKLE

I used to tickle you.
Do you remember?
you were a calf leaping
from her stall, your
soft, milky blue eyes following
the kaleidoscope of colors
on the mobile above you.
and I would reach down
to the warm pink of your belly,
gentle, teasing, dancing.
Your laughter was proof to me
that God exists.

SONG FOR A SOUL FRIEND

You are the shape of the forest's song.
You are the sky-hills of the swallow's flight,
a calligraphy of pine, and navy wings.
You paint the world from branch
to branch,
in gentle, swooping lines.

You are the hymn
of the fox burrow,
the dappled light, the crisp-crunch of leaves,
the walls a paper lantern, with
ember-fur as flame.
You are the pebble-shape of
their sleeping, and
the playful curve of their shoulders, just before
they leap into the snow.

You are the chorus
of the trees, in spring.
The wind sighs, and you sway,
your hands
the hands of an artist, brushing the sky;
sometimes outstretched, and sometimes,
softly cupped,
fingers laced in a delicate
crib of leaves.

You are the shape of the forest's song.
You are its stillness,
its wildness,

its wisdom,
its joy.

You are the shape
of the forest's song.

www.ingramcontent.com/pod-product-compliance
Lightning Source LLC
Chambersburg PA
CBHW060421050426
42449CB00009B/2064